HOW TO BE A GOOD GERMAN SHEPHERD DOG

"Self-Help For The Confused"

Lucy Olsen, GSD

Copyright © 2017 Gwynneth Mary Lovas

NOTICE AND DISCLAIMER: All rights reserved. No part of this publication may be reproduced, stored in a retrieval system, or transmitted, in any form or by any means, electronic, mechanical, photocopying, recording or otherwise, without the prior written consent of Gwynneth Mary Lovas.

This book is a work of fiction. Names, characters, places and incidents either are products of the author's imagination or are used fictitiously. Any resemblance to actual events or locales, dogs or persons, living or dead, is entirely coincidental.

This book is for entertainment purposes only. It is not for purposes of selecting or training German Shepherd Dogs, correcting behavioral issues with German Shepherd Dogs or encouraging or discouraging the ownership of German Shepherd Dogs.

LIMITATION OF LIABILITY AND DISCLAIMER OF WARRANTY: The Author makes no representation or warranty with respect to the accuracy or completeness of the contents of this book and specifically disclaims all warranties including, without limiting the generality of the foregoing, warranties or fitness of the contents for any particular purpose. The information, advice and strategies contained herein are provided solely for the purposes of entertainment and with the understanding that if professional advice or assistance is required, the services of a competent professional expert should be sought. The author shall not be liable for any direct, indirect, punitive, special, incidental or other consequential damages arising directly or indirectly from any use of this material, which is provided "as is" and without warranties.

ISBN: 978-0-9958170-2-9

How To Be A Good German Shepherd Dog

This book is dedicated to German Shepherd Dogs the world over, who devote their lives to the service of family, community and country.

Lucy Olsen GSD

How To Be A Good German Shepherd Dog

TABLE OF CONTENTS

Dedication iii

I. INTRODUCTION (AND EXPLANATION) 1

II. GENERAL SOCIAL CONDUCT 4
   1. Choosing A Name 4
   2. Soiling 6
       a. In General 6
       b. Revenge Soiling 6
       c. Fun With Poop (and other horrors) 7
       d. Emergency Soiling 9
   3. Farting 10
   4. Chewing 11
   5. Consumption of Food and Beverage 12
       a. What to Eat and Drink 12
       b. Table Manners 17
   6. Interactions With Your Master 19
       a. Identifying The Master 19
       b. Training 20
       c. General Rules 22
   7. Interactions With Other Humans 23
   8. Interactions With Canines 24
   9. Interactions With Non-Canines 26
  10. Speaking 28
  11. Going For A Walk 31
  12. Playing 33
  13. Exercise 34
  14. Grooming 35
  15. Visiting The Vet 36
  16. Romance 37
  17. Clothing 38
  18. The Kennel 39

III. THE INTERNATIONAL ORDER OF GERMAN
    SHEPHERD DOGS CODE OF CONDUCT 42
    1. Preamble 42
    2. Duties and Responsibilities 42
    3. Ethics 43
    4. Transgressions, Offences and Punishment 45
    5. How To Become A Member 46

IV. DEAR LUCY 47
    1. Introduction 47
    2. Letters 47
    3. How To Contact Lucy For Advice 50

V. THE GERMAN SHEPHERD DOG SONG 51

VI. A SPECIAL NOTE TO OUR MASTERS 53

About The Author 54

I. INTRODUCTION (AND EXPLANATION)

I am Lucy Olsen, GSD, and you may know me from my Mom's book, *The Retirement Diaries*®, published in 2016.

Of course you know who you are, Brigid in Boston, Fritz in Frankfurt, Monty in Manchester, Duke in Denver and Trixie in Toronto, to name a few.

The question is, are you good German Shepherd Dogs, or are you confused?

As you are no doubt aware, there are hundreds of books out there for your Masters to read and study that provide all sorts of information on what to feed you, how to train you and what physical and personality traits to look for in German Shepherd Dogs. But this is not a book for your Masters.

This is a book for you, my fellow German Shepherd Dogs, written by a German Shepherd Dog.

In much the same way that your Masters pour over self-help books, fashion catalogues and personality and life-style quizzes in magazines seeking to understand and better their personal behavior and appearance, this book was written with your personal betterment in mind.

You see, contrary to popular belief, being a good German Shepherd Dog can't always be determined by your lineage, your cost, or even your rakish good looks.

It's also not easy to tell how good you are at being a German Shepherd Dog based only on the way your Master treats you. Let's face it, those big pink tongues, dewy eyes, velvety ears, handsome coats and giant paws make us pretty adorable to our Masters from the moment they first lay eyes on us. To say nothing of our indomitable spirits, innate alertness and intellectual horsepower, which only serve to make it virtually impossible for our Masters to make any kind of accurate assessment regarding how good we are at being German Shepherd Dogs.

Some of us are even quite snappy dressers, which makes evaluating us even more difficult. Of course when I say "snappy dressers" I'm referring to collars, work vests and leashes here - we are not Yorkshire Terriers. But, while these accessories to our natural beauty can make us even more "good looking", even they aren't much of an indication as to whether or not we are actually good at being German Shepherd Dogs.

The sad truth is, while we may all have the potential to be the most precocious playmates at the park, the stars of our local annual Schutzhund demonstrations or Best In Show at any number of prestigious dog spectacles, I have personally witnessed and heard rumors (unfortunately supported by photographic and video evidence) suggesting that a few of you GSDs out there have lapsed into conduct unbecoming or detrimental to the dignity of your fellow GSDs. That's right, I'm talking about the excessive tail-wagging, silly hijinks, costume-wearing and ridiculous antics that for some strange reason seem to endear us to our Masters and end up being memorialized for all eternity on YouTube.

All German Shepherd Dogs deserve to know the truth. Certain behaviors are totally inappropriate for German Shepherd Dogs. And, while most of us will inherently sense when we are being asked to behave and perform in ways that go entirely against our nature, some of us just want to please our Masters so much that we ignore our instincts, and allow our Masters to cross that line between encouraging appropriate German Shepherd Dog behavior and expecting us to engage in activities that should really remain the domain of certain Labra Doodles, Chihuahuas and Toy Poodles.

My goal is to help all GSDs understand their true nature and purpose, and to encourage appropriate behavior that will demonstrate to our Masters where the line should be drawn between a Master's obsessions with Facebook and "matching" Halloween outfits, and our dignity as a truly noble breed of dog.

I have therefore taken it upon myself to write what is really a German Shepherd Dog self-help book, so that none of us ever again allow ourselves to be coerced into "mastering" inane tricks or posing for photographs wearing "funny" hats, sunglasses or costumes of any kind whatsoever.

Every German Shepherd Dog deserves to know and understand how to be a good German Shepherd Dog, and to live up to the intended design of our creator, Max von Stephanitz:

"Remarkable in his unswerving loyalty to his Master, irrepressible in his high spirits, never idle, always in motion, good-natured but not a flatterer, a constant pleasure to the eye..."

It helps if you think of it this way; dogs that qualify as GSDs are the canine equivalent of people that qualify as PhDs.

II. GENERAL SOCIAL CONDUCT

1. CHOOSING A NAME

It all starts with your choice of name.

I know that we have no control over what our Masters name us. That is beside the point. Whether your Master has named you Bootsy, Puddles or Sneezy, you must choose your own name in keeping with the dignity of our breed.

It is advisable to adopt a name that is not too dissimilar from the name your Master calls you, although, for those of you called Popsicle, Twinkie and Fluffers, first of all, my sympathies, and secondly, I think you can just go with anything Germanic, or with a military, noble or authoritative connotation.

Sergeant, Duke, Elsa, Ludwig, Magda, Deputy, King, Franz, Rex, Hedda, Jack, Major, Conrad, Baron, Rudy, Hans, Lady, Fritz, Marshall, Prince and Schatze are all perfectly acceptable. The name I have chosen for myself, for example, is Lujza, which means "renowned warrior".

For those of you who wish to honor our creator when you adopt a new name, there can be no German Shepherd Dog name more befitting than Max, Maxine, Von or Stephan.

Once you have chosen your adopted name, the key is to then govern yourself accordingly. Notwithstanding the fact that your Master may have named you Booboo, you are to think of yourself and carry yourself as Rudy, Elsa, Duke or whatever other appropriate name you have chosen. At all times.

Should your Master yell, "Noodles!" (or anything else completely lacking in dignity) at the dog park, you are required, of course, to respond. Under no circumstances should you skulk, shrink, cry, run away or demonstrate in any way your level of embarrassment at the moniker. The shame, if any, belongs entirely to your Master, who really should know better than to allow a six-year-old to name a German Shepherd Dog.

It is your demeanor alone that will demand respect and dictate how other dogs will react when they notice you responding to the lady in the pink baseball cap shrieking, "Bubbles!" from across the field.

You must make it clear to all canine acquaintances from the get-go that your response when your Master calls, "Tootsie!" is purely a matter of chain-of-command obedience, and in no way signifies your acquiescence to the moniker. Under no circumstances are you to tolerate snickering, guffawing, eye-rolling or mocking of any sort by other canines if your Master calls out, "Nutso!", "Cookie!", or "Wiggles!" at the park.

At the first hint of disrespect from a fellow canine in the vicinity, I recommend a meaningful glance in the direction of said canine, accompanied by an almost imperceptible curl of the upper lip if you feel the situation warrants it.

Of course in order to pull this off, there can be no bouncing, flouncing, prancing, dancing, grinning, bowing or other silliness of any kind whatsoever when your Master calls you by the ridiculous name they have chosen.

If your Master shouts out, "Snickers!" in front of everybody, or even, "Mister Dinglebunny!", you are to simply stop what you are doing, turn to face your Master and move at an appropriate pace in the direction of your Master. You are to remain calm, alert and dignified.

In order to support your efforts in this respect, I can recommend a useful exercise. Whenever you have a spare moment or two, try repeating the silly name your Master has given you over and over in your head, followed by your chosen name.

It won't be too long before you will find that every time your Master calls out, "Cupcake!", your subconscious will actually hear the name "Chief".

2. SOILING

a. In General

"Soiling" includes every physical release of bodily material other than sneezing.

To be specific, if you find yourself squatting, lifting a rear leg, tucking your hind quarters beneath you in an "almost seated" position, or holding your jaw open in an exaggerated fashion while stretching your neck out and down, you are most likely either in the process of, or about to engage in, "soiling".

Subject to the limited qualifications laid out in the subsections below, as a general rule, soiling anywhere other than in an area designated or approved by your Master is strictly prohibited. Even when you are "almost positive" no one is looking.

Trust me. They are not going to blame the budgie, the cat or an "intruder" if they find a pile of poop beside their bed or a puddle of pee in the middle of the kitchen floor.

b. Revenge Soiling

Which brings us to the first of three specific categories of soiling that must be addressed separately.

We all know that "revenge soiling" is not an uncommon canine response when a dog's Master:

(i) Leaves him behind when the family goes out for a four hour drive on a sunny Sunday afternoon;
(ii) "Forgets" about him for sixteen hours because he or she wanted to "go for a drink" with his or her buddies straight after work;
(iii) Ignores the dog's need to play catch for eight days in a row despite frequent "hints" (physically placing a tennis ball in his or her lap) or
(iv) Gives too much attention to the cat, the girlfriend or the "new baby".

However, as instinctive a reaction as revenge soiling may be for certain "temperamental" breeds of dog (I think we all know who I'm talking about), it is unacceptable behavior in a German Shepherd Dog.

In addition to being completely counter-productive, revenge soiling is a clear indicator that a dog is putting its personal sensitivities and feelings ahead of service to its Master, which runs entirely contrary to appropriate German Shepherd Dog behavior.

c. Fun With Poop (and other horrors)

Although technically not so much a "soiling" issue as a "soiled" issue, it is worth mentioning in this chapter that dogs and humans are very different creatures when it comes to odors and our senses of smell.

Yes, everybody knows that dogs have a "better" sense of smell than humans, but if that were the real point, it would be the dogs who hold their paws over their noses every time Daddy farts, and not the other way around.

The point is that, as dogs, we can't help but be

fascinated by virtually every odor of every nature and kind whatsoever produced by anything organic. This includes the merely stinky or acrid, to the downright putrid.

We think nothing of sidling up to another dog and sniffing its bum, getting up close and personal with every freshly dropped stool at the dog park that takes our fancy ("Hmm. Yep. Thought so. Seamus had a piece of banana with his lunch."), lifting the cat's ass off the ground with our noses to get a better whiff of its anus, inhaling every trace of animal urine we encounter at the park, and rolling in the rotting carcasses of every recently or long-dead creature we can find. The rottener the better.

As dogs, we use our sense of smell for information gathering, in much the same way that our Masters use the internet. And there is a reason for this. For dogs, smell is a primal sense, enabling pleasure, warning us of danger, allowing us to find food, disguise our own scent, detect predators, and help us to locate Masters, friends, enemies, mates or virtually anything that we are trained by humans to locate by sense of smell.

Humans, however, have evolved to the point where they no longer rely on their sense of smell for such primal purposes.

That is why humans today require GPS to locate each other. Turn two dogs who want to find each other loose on the same continent, and they will find each other. Take their mobile phones away, and two humans can't even find each other in the same Walmart store.

It is also why we dogs can "smell the crazy" on the guy headed down the sidewalk towards our Master, while our Master is busy checking out his new Cabela jacket in every window we pass, and preoccupied with thoughts about where he should take his date for dinner.

But for humans, while their sense of smell can sometimes help them determine whether or not any food is "off", it is largely used as one of the many factors affecting their general sense of comfort. Smell can be either neutral, pleasurable or offensive to a human. That's right. Offensive.

While it may be difficult for dogs to even imagine what an "offensive" smell might be, as German Shepherd Dogs, you must be aware that certain odors can dramatically alter a human being's level of comfort. The mere fact that smell is "particulate" disturbs humans because, unlike us, they actually find the mere thought of inhaling molecules of someone or something else's bowel movement or rotting carcass rather disquieting.

Yes, difficult though it may be to believe, your Master actually does not appreciate it when your burps smell like dog poop or you have rubbed your face and neck into the rotting carcass of a dead bird.

Bearing in mind that service to our Masters is our prime directive as German Shepherd Dogs, we must, therefore, do everything in our power to refrain from bringing them any level of discomfort.

Which means, of course, that German Shepherd Dogs are prohibited from rolling in, playing with, munching on, "tasting" or purposefully stepping in excrement or detritus of any kind.

For the sake of complete clarity, this includes the contents of the cat's litter box.

d. Emergency Soiling

Incontinence or nausea caused by a medical condition, such as a urinary tract infection, diarrhea or the inadvertent ingestion of or exposure to a pathogen, are the only legitimate exceptions to the prohibition against soiling anywhere other than in an area designated or approved by your Master.

Note: This does not give you license to be lazy or simply "let fly" wherever you feel like it whenever you are feeling a little bit under the weather. A good German Shepherd Dog must still make every effort to do its soiling in appropriate areas.

Also note: While nervousness and "emotional upset" may be valid excuses for other breeds of dog, they do not qualify as "medical conditions" for German Shepherd Dogs. Snap out of it!

3. FARTING

Call it what you will, farting, passing gas, frabbing or whatever other name you might have for it, it is a perfectly natural and necessary bodily function for all mammals.

That said, bearing in mind your Master's sensitivity to certain types of odors, German Shepherd Dogs should politely excuse themselves from the media room when they sense a bout of gas coming on.

Should a fart sneak up on you and escape while you are in the company of your Master, you are required to have the dignity to own up to your faux pas. Trying to sneak silently out of the room, running in the opposite direction of the smell as though you have no idea where it came from and are "offended" by its very presence, signaling with your eyes that it was the cat that "did it" or feigning innocence in any other way is strictly prohibited and conduct unbecoming to a German Shepherd Dog. A good German Shepherd Dog always assumes responsibility for his or her own actions, whatever they may be.

In fact, there may even be situations in which you will be expected to "take one for the team", such as when Mommy and her boyfriend are snuggling on the couch and a malodorous emanation for which you are actually not responsible wafts through the room. A German Shepherd Dog should always be a good sport in such delicate situations.

4. CHEWING

Between the ages of two to twelve months, you baby teeth and adult teeth will be coming in, and you will be inclined to want to chew.

This is perfectly natural, and hopefully your Master will have provided you with appropriate items on which to chew during this time.

What, you may ask, are appropriate items? There is an easy way to tell whether or not the item on which you have decided to focus your chewing efforts is appropriate.

If your Master has given it to you, it is probably safe to assume that you are allowed to chew on it.

Note: While, technically speaking, your bed, your collar and your leash are "yours", they are not chew toys.

If an item you are eyeing is normally in a closet, on the sofa or on a bed, it is almost never an appropriate chewing item.

If it is made of wood or paper, is larger than a bread box, or your Master has ever worn it, it is definitely off limits.

If, every time you pick it up in your mouth, your Master says, "No" or "Off" in a very firm voice and takes it away from you, then you can consider that item permanently verboten.

If it can walk, swim, fly or crawl, has feathers, fur, skin or a detectable heartbeat, don't even think about it.

If it is attached to wiring of any kind, is made of metal or hard plastic, you have seen it "light up", or you have heard it beep, bleep, ping, talk, play music, show pictures, ring or make any sound other than "squeak", think very long and hard before picking it up in your mouth.

If merely seeing you with a specific item in your mouth has resulted in your Master fainting, screaming, bursting into tears or reaching for a weapon, you have certainly misjudged the "chewability" of the item in question, and should avoid going anywhere near it, or anything even remotely resembling it, for the duration of your existence on earth.

While other breeds of dog may engage in chewing "for fun" or to relieve boredom throughout their lives, past your teething stage, chewing is simply not essential to the well-being of a German Shepherd Dog, and is to be strongly discouraged.

But in all cases, chewing on anything other than an object designated or approved by your Master is strictly prohibited.

Note: The discovery of a leather slipper in the vicinity or your rawhide chew toy does not constitute "approval".

5. CONSUMPTION OF FOOD AND BEVERAGE

a. What To Eat And Drink

You require food and water to sustain life.

That said, the mere fact that you require them to remain alive does not entitle you to consume everything that will fit into your mouth whenever you feel the urge.

Consuming anything other than food or beverage designated, approved and served to you by your Master is strictly prohibited.

While, at first blush, the above may seem obvious, there are a number of circumstances in which it is not always easy for a dog, even a German Shepherd Dog, to grasp whether or not all four corners of the "test" have been satisfied prior to indulging.

You must, therefore, ask yourself these questions in advance of digging in:

(i) Has my Master designated this food as "mine"?
(ii) Has my Master "approved" my consumption of this specific food?
(iii) Has my Master (or his or her authorized delegate) "served" it? and
(iv) Has my Master served it "to me"?

In light of the fact that the permutations and combinations of answers to these questions can lead to confusion, a few exercises in applying this four-pronged test may prove beneficial.

First, certain foods will be specifically designated as "yours". The contents of that forty-pound bag of grain-free kibble on the landing to the basement, for example. How can you tell? Well, it will never appear on your Master's dinner plate or in the attractive little serving dishes and trays you will see laid out when guests arrive.

However, even though it may be food that has been designated as 'yours", you actually do not have license to tear open the bag and wolf down the contents willy-nilly whenever the urge strikes you. You are, in fact, required to wait until that designated food is served to you.

Neither does the mere fact that the cat has ripped open a large hole in said forty-pound bag and the contents have spilled out onto the floor satisfy the parameters of the test.

Although it may be arguable that the food on the floor has been "served", the fact that it is the cat that has "served" it fails to adhere to the requirement that the food must be served to you "by your master".

It is advisable to bear in mind that, while the cat is fully capable of giving the distinct impression that it is so authorized, and indeed may go so far as to take the liberty of exercising *de facto* control over your bag of food, it almost never has been granted the legally delegated *de jure* authority to serve food to you.

In much the same way, leaping up and helping yourself to whatever is on a kitchen counter, or conspiring with the cat to "serve" you whatever it can knock onto the floor, is conduct unbecoming to a good German Shepherd Dog. GSDs are encouraged to wait patiently for their Masters to serve them one of the cookies from the jar on the kitchen counter that have been designated as dog treats.

To delve a little more deeply into just how complex the issues surrounding the consumption of food can be, we should look at another example.

There will undoubtedly be numerous occasions when your Master will give you a piece of hamburger, steak, pizza, banana, carrot or some other delightfully tasty morsel.

It is clear, therefore, that while such foods may not necessarily be "designated" as your food, they can be "approved" for your consumption.

In light of the above, you may be surprised to learn that your Master is technically not serving an approved food "to you" when he leaves a platter of freshly barbequed steaks on the picnic table while he goes into the house to fetch a bottle of wine.

I warn you of this nuance in advance, as it can be a particularly troublesome lesson to learn "the hard way".

Furthermore, even though there will be occasions when your Master (or an authorized delegate) may hold an "approved" item out for you to take from their hand, or toss it in your general direction, you are to be strongly discouraged from assuming that, thereafter, every vaguely similar food item being held in a person's hand is yours for the taking. It is actually commonplace for a human to pick up and hold onto a food item in their hand without immediately devouring it.

And put away those stop-watches. There is no specific time limit for a human to hold said food item in their hand, after which you are entitled to assume it is "yours".

Nor may you resort to the 'oft used ruse employed by Golden Retrievers and their ilk of "accidentally" touching their noses to dangling food items in a devious and shameless attempt to encourage the human to either drop whatever is in their hand, or outright cede ownership of the item in question.

Certain other breeds of dog (which shall remain nameless) have even been rumored to go by what they euphemistically refer to as the "finders keepers" rule. There is no such rule. It has been fabricated by hustlers and scavengers, and it is to be neither adopted nor encouraged by German Shepherd Dogs. Anything on the floor is not necessarily "up for grabs".

Don't encourage bad feeding habits. The only one who will suffer will be you.

When in doubt of any kind, a useful rule of thumb to be employed is, if the food in question has been placed by your Master in "your" dish (not to be confused with "a" dish), or it is being directly handed or tossed to you while your Master is making eye contact with you, then that particular item has been served "to you" for your guilt-free consumption.

Hint: "Your" dish is almost always the one on the floor. Not to be confused with the gravy-filled stainless steel roasting pan sitting on top of the stove.

Note: Although they may technically be "close" to the floor, greasy dinner plates resting in an open dishwasher are also not "yours".

In addition, while other members of the family in your charge may have the delegated authority to feed you, it is very rare for a toddler to be permitted such rights. Therefore, a word of caution is warranted about anything the toddler drops into your dish.

Toddlers are notoriously unreliable at discerning what is appropriate to put in their own mouths, let alone yours. They are just as likely to drop one of Daddy's good socks, the cat or a picture frame into your dish, as a soda cracker. Govern yourself accordingly.

Warning: Do not, under any circumstances, allow yourself to be tempted by a hunk of raw meat being flung anonymously into the yard whilst you are on duty. The likelihood that a piece of meat falling into your lap from the sky is a miracle, an entertaining and ingenious new way your Daddy has come up with to feed you, or the act of a kindly and well-meaning neighbor lady, is very slim.

Such tactics are most frequently employed by ne'er-do-wells who mean harm to you and your family. Therefore, should steak, chicken, sausages, or even bacon, suddenly "fall from the sky", immediately assume DEFCON 1 maximum security and readiness protocols. You are officially at "Cocked Pistol".

A final comment on appropriate food consumption: Despite the fact that it is in a dish and on the floor, the cat's food is off limits. And while I could spend some time discussing the importance of not eating the cat's food, my experience thus far has been that cats are not shy about enforcing this rule themselves, should you display any interest whatsoever in what is in their dish.

Although we have focused primarily on food consumption so far, it is also worthwhile mentioning a few simple rules when it comes to beverages.

Unless you are on liquid medication, the only liquid you should be consuming is water.

Note: Despite your Teutonic ancestry, don't kid yourself. Beer is not simply "better tasting" water.

I know it can "take the edge off". However, as much as you might occasionally dream about what "fun" it would be to have the charm and social skills of a Pug, even if only for just a few hours, remember this: Nobody is ever counting on a Pug to bring down an armed robber, locate a missing child, pull an injured civilian from a collapsed building, detect explosives or guard anything or anybody.

To say nothing of the fact that there is very little in life that is more pitiable than an intoxicated German Shepherd Dog sprawled on his or her back in the middle of a yard, belting out "Feelings" with mournful howls.

Moreover, as with food, it is important that you stick to the water your Master puts in your dish or squirts into your mouth at the dog park.

Note: The toilet bowl is not just another one of "your" dishes. Same applies to the wading pool, the bird bath and the sippy-cup the toddler has dropped onto the floor.

b. Table Manners

Having dealt with the question of "what" you can consume, your training would be incomplete without a word or two about general table manners.

The "to do" list of manners is short, and really largely focused on your general health and well being: wait until you are served, eat slowly and be sure to chew.

The "what not to do" list, however, is somewhat more comprehensive:

(i) While German Shepherd Dogs have internal clocks that are hard-wired to "mean solar time" at the Royal Observatory in Greenwich, London, unless your Master is known for literally forgetting to feed you, it is impolite to make a habit out of "signaling" whenever your dinner time is approaching. This includes circling your dish, jumping up and down in your dish, pawing at your Master's leg, laying your head forlornly on your Master's thigh while sighing, standing beside the bag of kibble and barking every three seconds until you get fed and picking your dish up in your mouth, physically carrying it over to your master and dumping it at his or her feet;

(ii) As challenging as it may be to contain yourself, try to avoid micromanaging the filling of your food dish. Your Master knows how much to feed you. And, "Supersize Me!" is not an appropriate element of a German Shepherd Dog's lexicon;

(iii) Between the moment that your Master has filled your dish with food and the moment that the dish is actually placed on the floor in your dining area, any whirling, twirling, crying, whining, barking, jumping up and down and spinning in circles with excited anticipation is to be strongly discouraged. As is the exaggerated yawning you do in a feeble attempt to pretend you aren't even paying attention to the preparation of your dinner. Your Master knows precisely what you are up to, and that you aren't even remotely bored or sleepy. Have some dignity. The cat is always watching;

(iv) For any number of reasons, inhaling your dinner is to be frowned upon. Refer to the "to do" list for details;

(v) Unless you are actually choking on your food, loud gagging is looked upon as rude in most circles;

(vi) Slobbering, drooling, playing with, spraying or in any way creating a scene with your food is unacceptable. Your dining area should never appear to beg the question, "Who flung dung?" and

(vii) Nosing your empty dish all around the floor after eating your dinner suggests one of two things; either your Master has "made a mistake" when measuring out your food, or you are greedy. In either case, the message is unsettling and inappropriate. German Shepherd Dogs do not do "seconds" or "afters".

Lastly, just a quick word about water manners.

No one is going to believe that your two front paws ended up in your water dish "accidentally".

6. INTERACTIONS WITH YOUR MASTER

a. Identifying The Master

As a German Shepherd Dog, you are, by nature, exceptionally intelligent, loyal, and versatile.

Notwithstanding the fact that German Shepherd Dogs can deduce in about three seconds who the Master (read "alpha") in a house is, for reasons beyond our comprehension, humans think they can simply "elect" or "choose to be" the Master in a house. Or worse, pretend that everybody in the house has the same status.

While we can agree that everybody in the house may have equal rights, and that we are responsible for the care, protection and well-being of every member of our household, we know that everybody is actually not a born leader, alpha or Master. We are also aware that just because you are the one who paid for us or brought us home doesn't necessarily make you the Master.

That said, the issue only really tends to come up when we receive conflicting information, signals or commands from different members of our families.

In such cases, our every instinct will be to give the greatest "weight" to the information, signal or command emanating from the actual alpha, whom we will have identified from day one of our tenure with a family.

The rule is this: Follow that instinct.

Pay attention to the *de facto* alpha when faced with conflicting information, signals or commands, notwithstanding which family member believes themselves to be the alpha, talks the loudest, feeds you the most frequently, gives you the greatest number of treats, lets you lie on the sofa or picks up your poop from the yard.

The security and well-being of the entire family depends upon the security and well-being of the alpha/Master, and that, therefore, is your prime directive.

b. Training

It is from your Master that you will learn how you are expected to conduct yourself within the family and what particular needs and expectations your Master has of you.

When well-socialized and well-trained, you can learn

and do almost anything that doesn't absolutely require opposable thumbs, and it is your Master who will undertake your socialization and training.

As a German Shepherd Dog, the expectations will invariably be high, and you are therefore required to pay very close attention.

In the beginning, you will be trained with a combination of verbal commands, hand signals and possibly micro facial expressions and/or other signals. You will be fully trained when you are so in tune with your Master that the verbal commands are no longer required in some circumstances.

There may even be situations where you will be required to act based on your training and instinct without the benefit of any kind of command.

In addition, your Master is entitled to determine the full nature and extent of physical contact with you that is necessary and appropriate for your training, grooming or any other purpose that he or she deems necessary.

No, this does not give you license to reciprocate.

Yes, this includes affixing the protective cone around your head that was prescribed by the vet to prevent you from injuring yourself following your "you know what" surgery.

No, I don't know why it is called the "cone of shame".

No, your undertaking to not to lick yourself isn't good enough.

All physical contact with you by your Master must be borne with tolerance, acceptance and grace.

Exception: Any attempt at physical contact with you that poses an unwarranted threat to you or to your ability to fulfill your duties and obligations to those in your charge must be challenged, but only by such use of force as is essential to protect yourself and mitigate the threat.

c. General Rules

Sometimes you can be too smart for her own good.

Just because you have grasped that Daddy always gives you the commands to "sit", "lie down", "stay" and "rollover" in the same order fifty times a day, you are not allowed to start "cutting to the chase" and going straight into a "rollover" the moment he starts your lessons.

It will make Daddy feel like you have outsmarted him. And you will not get a treat.

While this is not meant as a criticism, you can have a tendency to be almost evangelical about your innate appreciation for how certain things - which includes almost everything - "should" be done. As far as you are concerned, there is "your" way, and then there is the "wrong" way.

That said, when you notice your Master doing things the "wrong" way, whether it is washing your food dish, putting on your collar or even feeding the cat, you must not, under any circumstances, look at your Master as if you are thinking, "…amateur."

Your Master will know what you are thinking. You never want to make your Master feel like you look on him or her as the trailer park parent of a child prodigy.

It is also worth taking into consideration the fact that not everything your Master does in life is meant to be a training session for you.

If he or she forgets to pick up the poop in the yard for a day or two, your Master doesn't necessarily expect you to "take over" that function.

Without opposable thumbs, a plastic bag or a scooper, you are going to be reduced to picking the poop up with your mouth and piling it in a corner on the back deck.

As delighted as you may be with your accomplishment,

your Master is quite possibly going to have a completely different reaction.

And finally, we all know that German Shepherd Dogs are capable of mastering the Jedi Mind Trick. We also know that the Force can have a powerful effect on weaker minds, allowing those who have mastered it to take advantage of others by implanting suggestions in their minds.

There are no circumstances in which you are permitted to use the Jedi Mind Trick on your Master.

Not even if it is "for his own good".

The use of your power should be reserved for hooligans and baddies.

Trust me. It may work for a while, but soon enough your Master will put two and two together and realize that there can be nothing other than mind control to account for the fact that his or her hand reaches into your treat jar to give you a cookie forty-eight times a day.

7. INTERACTIONS WITH OTHER HUMANS

How you interact with other humans will depend, to some extent, on your job.

But in all cases, your physical appearance and fearless, direct expression alone are imposing enough to be an effective deterrent to minor unwanted interference with you or those in your charge.

It is, therefore, not necessary to present your hard-tempered, business-like side for all human interactions unless you are fulfilling protection, police or military responsibilities.

While your personality should not lend itself to immediate and indiscriminate friendships, you should have sufficient self-confidence to stand your ground and meet overtures from other humans without expressing hostility or appearing nervous or skittish.

You should not, however, make overtures to other humans.

"Watch And Wait" should be your motto.

Although it should go without saying, I will say it anyway. Jumping upon, barreling into, pawing, licking and sitting upon humans of any size without provocation is strictly prohibited.

Notwithstanding all of the above, you will always alert your Master and those in your charge when any unknown human is about to breach the security perimeter you have established. See section 10, "Speaking" for full details.

Finally, any human your Master has permitted within said security perimeter will operate freely, but always under your strict surveillance.

8. INTERACTIONS WITH CANINES

Your Master will, quite rightfully, have every expectation that you will develop, with his or her advice and assistance, the normal social skills appropriate to encounters with other canines.

That said, normal social skills for a German Shepherd Dog do not (and should not) even remotely resemble normal social skills for a Labrador Retriever, a Boxer, a Shih Tzu or a West Highland Terrier, to say nothing of a canine of unknown ancestry (commonly referred to as a "Mutt").

You are not bred to be "the life of the party". Your demeanor should not scream, "Whoopee! Hijinks!" when you step into a room.

You are never going to have, nor do you want to have, two thousand friends on Facebook.

You won't have to worry about huge long-distance phone bills every month or be concerned about your "roaming" charges when you are away from home. The other dogs are simply not going to be falling all over themselves trying to "keep in touch" with you.

And don't expect your acquaintances from the dog park to remember your birthday, send you a Valentine's Day card or even share their toys or treats with you.

It is also extremely unlikely that they will ever be inspired to salute you with a "chest bump", a "high five", a "Nice to see you again!" or even a broad smile when you arrive on the scene.

These truths could be interpreted as the "down" side of being a natural-born working dog.

On the "plus" side, however, that same *gravitas* that is inextricably linked to your physical presence and essentially precludes your nomination for the "Miss Congeniality" Award, will normally be of tremendous assistance in helping you perform whatever duties you have been assigned. There is every likelihood that you will always be taken seriously by other canines. Usually very seriously.

In light of the above, the most important rule for you to remember about interactions with other canines is this: Unwarranted aggression towards any other canine will not be tolerated. If you can memorize this one rule, you will be fine.

For greater certainty, the following situations do not "warrant" aggression:

    a. Your master has petted, praised, or given a treat to another canine;

b. Another canine at the dog park has unwittingly picked up the very stick you had been keeping an eye on;
c. Another canine has erroneously assumed that your Master was tossing the tennis ball "for everybody" at the park;
d. Another canine, having accompanied his or her Master to your Master's house for a human get-together, has either inadvertently looked at your food dish, licked one of your toys, wandered too close to your bed or assumed that he or she was entitled to relieve him or her self in your yard or
e. Another canine lives in the house with you and is either eating "wrong", having fun "wrong", going up the stairs "wrong", sleeping "wrong", drinking "wrong", or simply not living up to your expectations of appropriate behavior.

That said, your threat assessment skills are second to none, and under no circumstances should you be shy to use your formidable physical and mental capabilities to oppose and put down any serious threat to your Master, to one of your charges or to yourself from another canine.

9. INTERACTIONS WITH NON-CANINES

When warranted, you may be required to prevent injury to others by a dangerous non-canine that has the capability of inflicting serious harm (think bear, snake, cougar, alligator, wild boar). In such circumstances, a good German Shepherd Dog will not hesitate to act.

However, unwarranted physical interaction by you of any nature or kind whatsoever, including, without limiting the generality of the foregoing, chasing, pawing, biting, mouthing, licking, playing with and tossing, either cats, skunks, porcupines, deer, squirrels, mice, lizards, horses, gerbils, chipmunks, rabbits, birds, bears, frogs, cows, snakes or turtles, is strictly prohibited.

Tempted though you may sometimes be, any such interaction serves only as a distraction from your prime directive, and may result in injury to one or both of you, or to toxic levels of exposure on your part to quills, venom or tomato juice.

Punishment for any transgression of this rule will be meted out in accordance with the magnitude of the transgression, which is directly proportional to the relationship between your Master and the non-canine in question.

You will, therefore, want to pay close attention to the following "annotations".

If your Master has ever fed, played with, kissed, petted or groomed the non-canine in question, any transgression, no matter how minor, will not be taken lightly.

If there is a framed photograph of said non-canine on the mantel above your Master's fireplace, and your transgression has resulted in any kind of injury to the creature, you will want to give serious consideration to operating in stealth mode for several hours, if not days.

If, as a result of your transgression, the following five criteria have been met, my recommendation would be to pack up your leash, your dish and your bed and scour the "Pets Wanted" section of the Classifieds in your local newspaper:

    a. The non-canine has expired;
    b. You are not injured;
    c. The non-canine had a "name";

d. The non-canine had a bed, a cage, a blanket, a dish, a collar or a "box of toys" in your Master's house and
e. Upon witnessing the transgression, your Master has started screaming unintelligibly and/or suffered a myocardial infarction.

To reiterate, unwarranted physical interaction by you of any kind with any non-canine creature is strictly prohibited.

Notwithstanding all of the above and, yes, perhaps ironically, you are expected to tolerate, with as much stalwart dignity and composure as you can muster, all non-lethal interference with your person instigated by the cat, the bird, the gerbil, the hamster, the gecko or the bunny.

Note: The "killer rabbit" defense will be of no assistance whatsoever should "Marshmallow" and "Flopsy" be discovered in a pool of blood under the dining room table. Humans are aware that there are no such things as "killer rabbits". They are Monty Python creatures of fiction.

Also note: Disconcerting though it may be, the "lethal interference" standard is not met when Elvis the budgie does a "fly by", or lands on your nose and poops.

Finally, while the cat may actually intend "lethal interference" when it leaps out at you from behind a closet door, it has a tendency to seriously overestimate its own capabilities and underestimate yours. It is normally unnecessary for an encounter with a five-pound mountain lion "poseur" to end in tragedy.

10. SPEAKING

"Speaking" refers to making any sound through your mouth, including barking, yipping, whining, growling, howling, sighing, crying and "talking".

Note: As they are not within your physical control, belching and sneezing are excluded from this definition.

Also Note: Singing is permissible, but only when you are singing *The German Shepherd Dog Song* as set out in Chapter V.

While German Shepherd Dogs have every tendency to lean towards being "vocal", my recommendation is that, to the greatest extent possible, you reserve your vocalizations for specific purposes. Remember, you are not a Miniature Schnauzer. There is a reason why seventy-two percent of Miniature Schnauzers are named "Barkley".

That said, there are, of course, those of you who feel compelled to provide a full "SITREP" every time your Master or one of your charges returns from "being away".

Understandably, you are not fully comfortable when your Master, in particular, but really any one of your charges, has wandered outside the "circle of love" you have created for them.

These reports, although not always warranted (Mommy doesn't really need to "know" that Daddy made a sandwich while she was gone), can be a part of your duties and provide important information in certain cases.

I recommend delivering them with as many nuances in inflection, tone and volume as possible, beginning with the more significant elements of the report ("Three strange men wearing balaclavas tried to break down the back door"), and ending with those aspects of your day that are really not all that pertinent to your duties or, to be completely truthful, to anyone but you ("The cat was mean to me").

In general, though, all vocalizations should be appropriate to their purpose.

Just as an example, while a short, single bark to signal

that you need to go out to the yard or come back into the house may be appropriate, incessant howling or crying at the back door is completely unnecessary, particularly if accompanied by any other weird behavior such as leaping up and throwing your full body weight at the patio door over and over again until you get a response.

If there is no emergency, "speak only when spoken to" is not a bad rule of thumb.

Note: No matter how many stories you are dying to tell her, simply overhearing your granny's voice on speakerphone does not constitute "being spoken to".

Speaking to any extent should, in general, be reserved for alerting your Master or those for whom you are responsible of a potential threat or danger.

Potential threats should be dealt with according to the Threat Level into which they fall.

A squirrel, cat or high wind in the backyard is a Threat Level One, and requires nothing more than that you "keep an eye" on the situation.

Unfamiliar noises constitute a Threat Level Two and a certain degree of heightened readiness on your part.

Familiar canines or humans approaching the security perimeter are a Threat Level Three, and require your full attention in anticipation of a breach of the perimeter.

Unfamiliar human females rate a Threat Level Four, and you are encouraged to make your presence known to them without necessarily sending out an alarm to your Master. A low, muffled sound or two usually does the trick, particularly when accompanied by a fixed stare. Although, as long as you can be certain that you have been seen, sometimes silence can be more threatening than any vocalization.

When faced with a Threat Level Five, such as an unfamiliar canine accompanied by a familiar human, you will want to pump up the volume so as to discourage the canine from assuming any liberties inside your territory.

An unfamiliar, unaccompanied canine is a Threat Level Seven, and you cannot under any circumstances permit it to cross your perimeter without making it extremely clear that it is crossing into territory that is under the aegis of a German Shepherd Dog. While many of you may have actually begun your day at this state of readiness, you are now officially at DEFCON 4, and increased intelligence watch and strengthened security measures are required. Loud barking permitted.

Threat Level Eight mobilization readiness is reserved for unfamiliar human males, and you are now required to officially alert your Master that you are at DEFCON 3.

Anything travelling at unacceptable speed directly towards your Master or anyone in your charge is a Threat Level Nine, and you must assume that DEFCON 2 readiness protocols are in order. You and your Master must be ready to mobilize and engage the threat. Sound the alarm!

But save your most audacious guarding and protecting behavior for a Threat Level Ten danger.

Maximum readiness is required when an attack by unknown assailants is imminent, and you must provide an appropriate alert to your Master and put the perpetrators on notice that you are now at DEFCON 1 and will take all necessary measures to neutralize and terminate the threat.

11. GOING FOR A WALK

For most canines, "going for a walk" means accompanying their Master or other family members on an outing around the neighborhood.

This activity is invariably conducted with the canine attached to a leash or lead.

The purpose of said outing is usually threefold:
a. Allow the canine to relieve itself;
b. Provide moderate exercise for both the humans and the canine and
c. Engage in social activity if the opportunity presents itself.

As a matter of course, the typical canine will, during such excursions:
a. Wander aimlessly around the vicinity of the humans, guided solely by the length of the leash and whatever distractions catch his or her fancy, be they smells, sounds, wind-swept leaves, flowers, squirrels, birds or snow flakes;
b. Pay little, if any, attention to the humans unless "prompted" by a tug on the leash and
c. Excitedly welcome with wagging tail and high-pitched whining all other humans and canines encountered during the outing, straining at the end of the leash to engage in petting and/or playing sessions.

A German Shepherd Dog accompanies their Master or other family members on an outing around the neighborhood either on or off lead.

The purpose of an on-lead outing for a German Shepherd Dog is also threefold:
a. Allow you to relieve yourself;
b. Provide moderate exercise for your humans, and an opportunity for you to patrol the neighborhood at heal, constantly scanning as you conduct a Threat Level Assessment in real time and
c. Enable you to alert your Master to any existing threats to the neighborhood.

The purpose of an off-lead outing is identical to that of an on-lead outing, but with one addition:

d. Allow you to conduct more extensive reconnaissance and surveillance activities, establishing a broader security perimeter, searching out persons or property in need of protection or assistance and eradicating any existing threats to the security of the neighborhood.

As a matter of course, a good German Shepherd Dog should, during such excursions:

a. At all times remain cognizant of the precise location of, and any threats to, their Master;
b. Be on the lookout for and track any unfamiliar persons, animals, smells, sounds or movements in the neighborhood;
c. Alert their Master and neighbors to any threat detected and
d. Eliminate or neutralize all threats.

The bottom line? For the typical canine, the word "walk" signifies fun.

For the German Shepherd Dog, the word "walk" should signify an opportunity to fulfill one of your responsibilities.

12. PLAYING

Playing encourages appropriate social skills and determines your position in the pecking order.

Just kidding! After you have spent your first eight weeks playing with your litter-mates, you already know where you fit in any canine pecking order.

German Shepherd Dogs don't want or need to "play" with other dogs. Playing is a distraction from your duties.

If your first thought when you wake up every morning is, "Golly, I hope I get to play with Charlie today, he's so much fun", you probably have a little Jack Russell Terrier or Springer Spaniel in your DNA.

The only "playing" German Shepherd Dogs want to engage in is any activity with our Masters which, call it what you will, really boils down to exercise and training.

13. EXERCISE

German Shepherd Dogs were bred to work all day long.

We need lots of outdoor exercise for physical and mental conditioning.

We are strong athletes, and thrive on challenging activities and exercise.

Just as important as physical exercise, German Shepherd Dogs require mental exercise.

In addition to advanced obedience and agility classes, I highly recommend Schutzhund, a dog sport developed in Germany in the early 1900s as a German Shepherd Dog breed suitability test.

Schutzhund will test the strength of your desire to work, your courage, intelligence, perseverance and your protective instinct.

It will also test and train you physically, and build your strength, endurance, agility, and scenting ability.

But of course not every German Shepherd Dog will actually be engaged in protection, police, military, herding or search and rescue work.

For some of you, your duties will be restricted to serving and protecting your family or household. And, whether they want it or not, your entire neighborhood.

Just because that strange guy wearing a hard hat is in Mrs. Smith's yard and not yours doesn't mean you aren't going to be keeping a very close eye on him.

"You're welcome, Mrs. Smith."

While advanced Schutzhund training may not be for you or your Master, a good half-hour of catch with a Frisbee or tennis ball a few times a day will work wonders for your mental and physical well-being. Combine that with a couple of neighborhood strolls and visits to the off-leash dog park, and you should be a very happy and healthy German Shepherd Dog.

14. GROOMING

A good German Shepherd Dog always sets a good example with his or her grooming.

Proper grooming includes:
a. Brushing your coat daily;
b. Brushing your teeth daily;
c. Cleaning the "eye-boogies" that collect in the corners of your eyes (as required);
d. Checking and cleaning your ears (as required);
e. Nail clipping (as required) and
f. Bathing (as required).

Note: German Shepherd Dogs are fearless. Remember this when Mommy brings out the nail clippers. Squealing, crying and running away are all frowned upon.

That said, there is no shame in holding your breath or closing your eyes during any of your grooming procedures, if you absolutely must.

Hint: Beware the cat seeking to "assist" with your grooming. It is usually a prelude to a complete role reversal in which you end up spending countless hours grooming the cat with your not inconsiderable tongue while it lollygags and stretches out in the sunniest spot on the carpet. And yes, that is where hairballs come from.

15. VISITING THE VET

The S.O.P. (Standard Operating Procedure) for visits to the vet is simple:

    a. Sit calmly at your master's side in the waiting room;
    b. Any lack of cooperation with the technician trying to get you to stand still on the scale while she weighs you, is unacceptable;
    c. Squealing like a sissy when the cat in the carrier on the floor across from you hisses, is to be avoided at all cost;
    d. When your name is called, calmly follow your master to the examining room;
    e. If you must walk past the cat in the carrier to get to your examining room, "skittering" frantically past it like you have suddenly discovered that you are walking on ice, will embarrass your Master;
    f. When the vet finally enters the examining room, remain calm;
    g. Intentionally staring into the vet's eyes in a threatening manner, growling under your breath, lifting your upper lip, snapping, snarling, biting and leaping off the examining table are all likely to end badly and are, therefore, verboten;
    h. Attempting to escape from the examining room is conduct unbecoming to a German Shepherd Dog;
    i. Barking desperately while attempting to escape from the examining room, is only acceptable if the clinic is on fire and you are trying to warn everybody;

j. Crying, sobbing, screaming, shrieking, wailing, howling or registering displeasure, annoyance, pain or sensitivity in any way whatsoever during the examination and/or immunization process is simply unnecessary, humiliating and a disgrace to German Shepherd Dogs everywhere and
k. Pulling your Master like an Iditarod sled towards the closest exit while he or she is trying to pay the bill is not appropriate German Shepherd Dog behavior. Knock it off!

16. ROMANCE

German Shepherd Dogs are a magnificent breed.

Let's face it, we got it goin' on with the physical stamina, the brains, the superhero skills, the beautiful coats, the perfect teeth, the attention-grabbing tails, erect ears, slim waists and full chests.

Of course every other dog is going to want to get a piece of that action. Why else do you think four out of every five dogs at the shelter is a "shepherd mix".

But there are rules.

For those of you who have been left "intact" specifically for breeding purposes, you are very special German Shepherd Dogs. You are so special, in fact, that your Masters have determined that your genes should be passed down to future generations of German Shepherd Dogs.

That was the good news.

The bad news? Well, having been selected for breeding purposes as specimens of uncompromising perfection, romance, as you may have come to think of it, will be out of the question.

Whether you are slated to be the sire or the dam, there will be no winking, wooing, romantic strolls through the park, long conversations over a bowl of kibble or any of the other intimacies that would normally accompany the "getting to know you" and "falling in love" processes.

As "intact" German Shepherd Dogs slated for breeding, your romantic interludes, if you could even call them that, will be more like brief, arranged, loveless marriages. Very brief. No care or thought will be given to whether or not you find the mate your Master has chosen for you even remotely sexy or appealing. And if everything "takes", there won't even be a second date. No phone calls. No postcards from distant lands.

For those of you who are still "intact", not so much because you have been specifically selected to pass down your genes, as because your Master is simply reluctant to alter "what God gave you", a few words of caution. Whether you are looking for a long-term commitment or a one-night stand, remember that five minutes of "fun" can lead to a lifetime of responsibility. And, while your physical and intellectual prowess may be clear, your offspring will only get half of their genes from you. Beautiful and sweet though they may be, Afghan Hounds are airheads. I'm just saying, it's something to think about.

As for the rest of you who cannot spread your seed or give birth, there is one rather obvious "up" side. With the consent of your Master and a willing partner, you can feel free to "have at it" should love come your way!

17. CLOTHING

There are only four acceptable accessories a German Shepherd Dog is permitted to wear.

They are: a collar with tags, a lead or leash, a harness and a working vest. For those of you who are members of military and police organizations, K9 tactical gear may also be worn as required.

Good German Shepherd Dogs do not need or yearn for "clothing", "outfits" or "costumes", all of which are better left for those dogs that perform for the amusement and entertainment of humans who "go" for that sort of thing.

German Shepherd Dogs serve the needs of their Masters, their communities and their countries and protect humans and their property.

We do not "do" *Britain's Got Talent*.

We do not dress up on Halloween.

We do not put on "elf" costumes for family Christmas card photos.

Never mind what "all the other dogs are wearing". You are a German Shepherd Dog, and owe it to yourself and to your breed to maintain a semblance of dignity that will go straight out the window the first time you even "wonder" how you'd look in a pair of black patent rain boots.

So. Are we clear? No sunglasses, wizard hats, tuxedos, bunny ears, Santa hats, superhero capes, bow-ties or sequined tutus.

Not even lederhosen.

Not even during Oktoberfest.

Seriously.

18. THE KENNEL

Yes, I have saved the worst for the last. And yes, it sometimes comes to this.

Life has it's challenges, and there is probably no

challenge greater for a German Shepherd Dog than to even think about spending a day away from their Master, let alone a week or more.

Unfortunately, there will very likely come a time in your life when, through no fault of your own, your Master will either be required to "go away" for business purposes or "need" a vacation from work.

As working dogs, it is difficult for German Shepherd Dogs to understand the human "need" to take a break from work. Left to our own devices, we would be working every minute of every day when we are not training, exercising, eating or sleeping.

Humans, on the other hand, lead far more complex lives than we German Shepherd Dogs, and seem to require occasional breaks from the stresses of their working lives.

Bearing that in mind, you should prepare yourself for the inevitable "visit" to the kennel.

It will feel very frightening and alien at first. You will assume that you are being abandoned and not know why. At the very least, it will feel like a stay at the kennel is punishment.

But it is not. In fact, it is a place where responsible Masters deposit you for one or more days in order to ensure your care and safety for a period during which your Master will not be able to look after your needs.

You will be given an enclosed space that will house you, your bedding, your dishes and, in the unlikely event you have any, your toys.

You will have access to the outdoors for the purposes of relieving yourself.

You will be provided with ample food, water and any medication that you may require.

You will be walked.

They will have something called "yard time", which is

largely designed for the more sociable breeds of dog, but in which you will be permitted to partake so long as you behave yourself in accordance with the rules set out in section 8 above, Interactions With Canines.

In addition, you are required to memorize these four rules that apply specifically to visits to the kennel:
   a. Under no circumstances are you to cry when Daddy drops you off and leaves you at the reception desk;
   b. While you will definitely want to "keep an eye" on things, you are not "in charge" of the kennel staff or the other canine guests;
   c. The kennel staff have the full delegated authority of your Master and are to be treated as your Masters while you are in their care and
   d. Do not do anything to embarrass* your Master or yourself during your stay. Mommy will probably need the services of the kennel again next year, and none of the alternatives to the kennel are good. (Remember when they asked Uncle Dave to take care of you for a week last year and he "forgot" to feed you for two days?)

* To be clear, all of the following would qualify as embarrassments:
(i)   Pulling the fire alarm;
(ii) Hiring yourself out as a body guard during yard time for extra food;
(iii) Recruiting other dogs to form your own gang;
(iv) Masterminding a plan to dig a tunnel under the yard to set all the dogs "free" and
(v)   Organizing a kennel-wide hunger strike.

So, now that that's all settled, should you find yourself at the kennel some day, just remember: behave yourself, chin up, chest out, remain alert and don't forget that Daddy will be coming back to pick you up and bring you home.

III. THE INTERNATIONAL ORDER OF GERMAN SHEPHERD DOGS CODE OF CONDUCT

1. PREAMBLE

Whether your assignment here on earth is police work, military operations, tracking, guiding the blind, drug or bomb detection, search and rescue, herding, avalanche rescue or family guardian, as a German Shepherd Dog you represent what has been the world's most superb, versatile and dependable breed of canine for more than one hundred years.

Your code of conduct is clear and uncompromising. Learn it. Live by it.

2. DUTIES AND RESPONSIBILITIES

German Shepherd Dogs shall, in accordance with the high degree of responsibility bestowed upon their breed, at all times fulfill any lawful duty imposed by their Masters, serve the community at large and protect all persons in their charge against illegal acts.

Service to the community includes assistance to those members of the community who by reason of personal, economic, social or other emergencies are in need of immediate aid.

In the performance of their duties, German Shepherd Dogs shall respect and protect their Master's dignity and maintain and uphold the rights of all Masters.

German Shepherd Dogs may use force only as directed and only to the extent required for the performance of their duties.

No German Shepherd Dog may inflict, instigate or tolerate any unnecessary act of harm, cruelty or other degrading treatment or punishment on any person or other living creature.

German Shepherd Dogs shall protect the health of persons in their charge and, in particular, shall take immediate action to secure medical attention whenever required.

German Shepherd Dogs shall respect the commands of their Masters, the law and this Code of Conduct. They shall also, to the best of their capability, prevent and rigorously oppose any violations thereof in accordance with the provisions herein, including enforcement of punishments against German Shepherd Dogs who are in contravention of this Code for first and second offences.

In the conduct of their services, all German Shepherd Dogs must:
a. Understand that their primary responsibility is to safeguard their Masters' lives and property, prevent offences and preserve peace and order and
b. Remain faithful in their allegiance to those in their charge and strive to attain excellence in the performance of their duties.

3. ETHICS

German Shepherd Dog ethical behavior comes from the values, attitudes and knowledge that guide the judgments of each individual German Shepherd Dog.

Each German Shepherd Dog has to make difficult decisions and complex choices every day, and those decisions and choices are to be made based on these eight guiding principles:

a. Accountability. Much like good people of every faith, you are answerable not only for your actions, but also for your omissions. That's right. Being distracted by a squirrel isn't an excuse for forgetting to keep an eye on the toddler.

b. Fairness. You are required to treat all those for whom you are responsible fairly, equally and with self-control, tolerance and courtesy, without any consideration as to who among them is inclined to give you the greatest number of treats.

c. Integrity. You must always do the right thing, whether or not any "reward" is being proffered.

d. Leadership. You must follow all legal commands of your Master, even when your instinct strongly suggests you do otherwise.

e. Selflessness. You are required to act in accordance with (i) the commands of your Master, (ii) in the public interest and (iii) in the interest of those in your charge regardless of any consequences to yourself.

f. Use of force. You will only use force as legally directed in accordance with your role and responsibilities, and only to the extent that it is necessary, proportionate and reasonable in all the circumstances.

g. Fitness for work. You will ensure that both you and your Master are fit to carry out your responsibilities. It is strongly recommended that you acquire a Kong, tennis ball or Frisbee for these purposes, and engage your Master in activities several times a day.

Interrupting prolonged napping sessions is not only permissible, but advisable. For the truly ambitious German Shepherd Dog and Master, we recommend Schutzhund training. Although originally developed to test the working abilities of German Shepherd Dogs, these days you may find yourself in classes with other breeds. Do not be distracted or "put off" by the presence of German Shepherd Dog "pretenders".

  h. Conduct. You will behave in a manner, whether on or off duty, which does not (i) bring discredit on those who are in your charge or on the German Shepherd Dog community as a whole, or (ii) undermine public confidence in German Shepherd Dogs.

4. TRANSGRESSIONS, OFFENCES AND PUNISHMENT

While you can be forgiven almost any transgression from this code until the age of approximately nine weeks, by which time your erect ears should signal to you and to those around you that you are now officially a German Shepherd Dog, any lapse in behavior from that point forward is an offence.

For those of you who may be slow learners (or simply not be the brightest bulbs on the tree), you are permitted one teaching reprimand for a misdemeanor, which consists of a single, sharp bark in your face.

Should you fail to heed that warning, the second level of permissible punishment is a swift, firm neck grab that forces you to instantly drop and roll onto your back.

German Shepherd Dogs do not get a "third chance".

Any third misdemeanor is punishable by never again being taken seriously by the German Shepherd Dog community, and by striking your name off the Master Membership List of the International Order of German Shepherd Dogs.

As harsh as this may sound, let's face it, if you can't get the message after two tries, there's probably a bit of Bichon Frise in your background, or some other cheerful, affectionate and sensitive breed of dog. You, my friend, are a "companion" animal, also known as a "pet".

For you, continuing to pretend to be a German Shepherd Dog is the equivalent of a human being who plays "air guitar" calling himself a "musician".

You will have a wonderful life filled with hugs, kisses, cuddles and treats.

But you are not a German Shepherd Dog.

5. HOW TO BECOME A MEMBER

These standards reflect the expectations that the International Order of German Shepherd Dogs has of all German Shepherd Dogs, regardless of their role in society.

The Master Membership List will be maintained online at theretirementdiaries.com

Any German Shepherd Dog wishing to be enrolled in the International Order of German Shepherd Dogs may do so by emailing your name, city of residence, job and optional photo to lucy@theretirementdiaries.com

Your name, city of residence, job and photo will be added to the online Master Membership List of the International Order of German Shepherd Dogs.

IV. DEAR LUCY

1. INTRODUCTION

Following are excerpts from my *Dear Lucy* advice column found at theretirementdiaries.com.

2. LETTERS

Dear Lucy,
 My Mommy and Daddy brought a cat into our house. It isn't leaving. What do I do?

Sincerely,
Prince in Portsmouth

Dear Prince,
 First of all, my sympathies. I understand that this can be a very trying time for you.
 We have a cat in our house. Well, it is either a cat or a dragon. They call it Twink. But it was here when I arrived, so I grew up with it. When I say "with it", I mean in the same house, not as "pals".
 My best advice is to remember that, as magical and powerful as cats may appear to be, I believe their powers to be largely an illusion, which is the product of an extensive use of smoke and mirrors, a certain amount of hypnotism and the occasional Jedi mind trick.
 Nonetheless, a healthy dose of caution should be

exercised at all times. Never underestimate a cat. Or your Master's affection for it.

There are really only two important rules to keep in mind when living with a cat.

First, never, ever, under any circumstances whatsoever, look a cat straight in the eye. If you find yourself grooming the cat with your tongue, "accidentally" spilling the bowl of popcorn in front of the cat or letting the cat use you as a giant heating pad, it is already too late. You have been hypnotized, and will be the cat's minion for life.

Finally, never cry in front of the cat. Such behavior will not only diminish your status in the household, it will actually alter the natural world order.

Dear Lucy,

Last night my Dad brought a woman home.

When it was time to go to bed, he took her in our room and shut the door, leaving me in the hallway all night.

She is still here. Do I need to find another Master?

Sincerely,
Axel in Annapolis

Dear Axel,

My advice is not to worry. I doubt very much that you are being, or even could be, replaced by this woman.

As crazy as it may seem to us, many humans appear to prefer to do their mating in private, which, from what I understand, can be a prolonged and awkward ritual.

That said, you may want to keep an eye open for signs that she is starting to show an unnatural interest in fetching the newspaper or patrolling the perimeter of the yard for intruders.

Should that happen, you and your Dad may have more on your hands than either of you had bargained for.

Dear Lucy,

The other day at the park I noticed lots of other dogs were wearing really pretty coats.

I am nine years old and don't have any pretty coats. Doesn't my Mom love me?

Sincerely,
Tara in Trenton

Dear Tara,

Tara, Tara, Tara. Have you not read my book? Good German Shepherd Dogs don't wear costumes.

I think your Mom is really smart to not dress you up. She seems to know that German Shepherd Dogs are beautiful just the way God and Max von Stephanitz made them.

You don't need to buy a pretty coat. You were born with one.

Nonetheless, I note that you are "getting on" in years, and may simply be feeling that your image needs a little "lift" or "enhancement".

If that is the case, after so many years of faithful service, I can see no problem with a minor indulgence if it makes you feel better.

So, the next time you accompany your Mom to the pet store, just nudge her over to the "fancy" dog collar aisle.

But if she succumbs, please do German Shepherd Dogs everywhere a favor and wear that rhinestone collar with dignity.

Remember, you are not a Poodle!

---

3. HOW TO CONTACT LUCY FOR ADVICE

If you would like to have your German Shepherd Dog's request to Lucy for advice published online, please send your submission to lucy@theretirementdiaries.com[1]

You will be notified if your submission has been selected for publication.

---

[1] Upon submission to Lucy of a request for advice, you agree to transfer and assign all right, title and interest in the Submission to Gwynneth Mary Lovas, including the common-law copyright to the Submission, all reproduction rights and the right to claim statutory copyright. It is understood and agreed that Gwynneth Mary Lovas may reproduce or resell the Submission in whole or in part in any format whatsoever without your prior written approval or knowledge. All right, title and interest in the Submission shall be and remain the property of Gwynneth Mary Lovas. You may not print, publish or use any portion of the Submission in any manner whatsoever without consent in writing from Gwynneth Mary Lovas. Upon completion and acceptance of the Submission by Gwynneth Mary Lovas, you waive all moral rights to the Submission, including, but not limited to, the right to attribution, integrity and association of a work. It is understood that Gwynneth Mary Lovas may, as she in her sole discretion deems appropriate, distort, mutilate or otherwise modify the Submission and use the Submission in association with any product, service, cause or institution.

V. THE GERMAN SHEPHERD DOG SONG

Although it is recommended to be sung in groups of three or more, solo performances can also be quite inspiring, particularly when accompanied by an obliging pianist.

You are encouraged to invite your Master to join in the refrain.

Canaries are also permitted to join in.

Cats and toddlers are permitted to observe.

THE GERMAN SHEPHERD DOG SONG
(Sung to the tune of "Jingle Bells")

I was patrolling in the park
For a baddie on the prowl
When I smelled him in the dark
And so I signaled with a growl.

My Master took me off my rope
And he told me to make haste
That baddie didn't have a hope
Because I was born to chase.

(Refrain)
Hey! GSDs, GSDs
We're smart as we can be
And we always get our man
Just like the R.C.M.P.

Hey! GSDs, GSDs
We're loyal and we're true
And if you're a baddie
We will get you and your crew.

Lucy Olsen GSD

I was home alone today
My Masters don't have an alarm
So I barked, "Please go away!"
When a burglar planned us harm.

But when he failed to take the hint
And tried to enter our back door
I made sure he did a stint
On our hardwood kitchen floor.

(Refrain)
Hey! GSDs, GSDs
We're smart as we can be
And we always get our man
Just like the R.C.M.P.

Hey! GSDs, GSDs
We're loyal and we're true
And if you're a baddie
We will get you and your crew.

VI. A SPECIAL NOTE TO OUR MASTERS

If you have ever owned a German Shepherd Dog, you probably know what happens from the moment the clock radio turns on in the morning.

Whether you have it set to talk-show banter or classical music, it doesn't matter. A German Shepherd Dog always hears *Reveille*. It is the German Shepherd Dog equivalent of the Bat Signal. If our eyes are open, we are already at DEFCON 4.

German Shepherds are working dogs. In fact, if you don't give us a job, we are likely to make up our own (and quite possibly assume some of your duties. "Is that the teenager acting up again, Mom? Don't worry – I got this!")

My point? Please let us know what it is that you would like us to do. We want to work. You can't ask too much of us. We need to keep busy, and we love a challenge. We need physical exercise and mental stimulation.

If you forget that it is time for us to exercise or eat, we will remind you. If you don't hear the footsteps crossing the lawn, we will alert you. If you don't smell the empty pan overheating on the stove, we will bring it to your attention. In addition to undertaking any tasks that you, our Masters, ask of us, we learn from our experiences and can anticipate your needs before you are even aware of them.

If you provide us with food, water, exercise and veterinary care when we need it, we will devote our entire lives to you and do whatever you ask. We will protect you and those you love to our last breath.

We are German Shepherd Dogs, and that is what we do.

ABOUT THE AUTHOR

Gwynneth Mary Lovas is the author of *Canadian Military Law: Morale and Welfare Operations* (Carswell, 2013) and *The Retirement Diaries®* (2016). She has been a member of the Law Society of Upper Canada since 1982, and spent the last twelve years of her legal career as a Department of Justice Senior Counsel providing advice to the Department of National Defence and the Canadian Forces. She currently works as a writer, lecturer and consultant, and owns and operates theretirementfairy.com, a web site dedicated to providing humorous retirement cards and gifts, and theretirementdiaries.com, a web site dedicated to humorous retirement stories based on her novel *The Retirement Diaries®* and on Lucy's advice column for German Shepherd Dogs.

www.ingramcontent.com/pod-product-compliance
Lightning Source LLC
Chambersburg PA
CBHW061252040426
42444CB00010B/2366